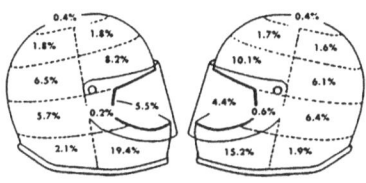

TRAJECTORY

✺

A VERSE BIOGRAPHY

OF EVEL KNIEVEL

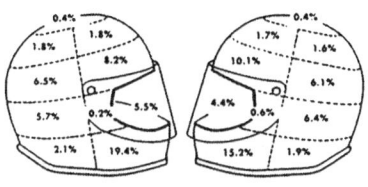

TRAJECTORY

❁

A VERSE BIOGRAPHY
OF EVEL KNIEVEL

❁

EMILY VIGGIANO SALAND

NEW MICHIGAN PRESS
TUCSON, ARIZONA

NEW MICHIGAN PRESS
DEPT OF ENGLISH, P. O. BOX 210067
UNIVERSITY OF ARIZONA
TUCSON, AZ 85721-0067

<http://newmichiganpress.com>

Orders and queries to <nmp@thediagram.com>.

Copyright © 2019 by Emily Viggiano Saland.
All rights reserved.

ISBN 978-1-934832-69-1. FIRST PRINTING.

Printed in the United States of America.

Design by Ander Monson.

CONTENTS

Of the Items Necessary: 1
This Was Not the Kind of Space 2
On the Day He Was Born the Sky Looked Like This: 4
As a Copper Mine Dreams of Surfacing 5
The Death of Robert Craig Knievel, Jr. 6
Caesar's Palace, 1967 7
Or Else Picture the Curve at the Nape of a Neck 8
Pity the Comet its Slow Descent 9
Meridian Idaho, 1968 10
Houston Astrodome, 1971 11
Cow Palace, 1972 12
Sky Cycle 13
"Good luck with your undertaking" 16
He Was Ever Some Sort of Scaffolding on the Sky 17
Snake River Canyon, 1974 18
Wembley, 1975 19
King's Island, 1975 21
1977 Shark Jump 23
With Apologies to Shelly Saltman 24
Remembering Always That the Last Two Fractures Were Obtained on the Golf Course and in the Bath 25
Clutch 26

Notes and Acknowledgments 29

OF THE ITEMS NECESSARY:

Of course the wind.

A horizon, birch-bent. Maybe two.
From the ground it looks like a rib,
from the sky—shadow of the same.

The motion of an object   in or through a medium
          (rephrase: the *sustained* motion).
Ascent.
Boundaries.

Need is a winged thing,
feathered, quill-hollow.

Let's not forget the roll, yaw, and pitch.

This poem is endless, as

the heart, a magpie squawking
after and after.

THIS WAS NOT THE KIND OF SPACE

> *b. October 17, 1938—Butte, Montana*

one could turn around in, stretch
and get comfortable. This was
suspension: uneasy in that it was indeterminate.

The launch, the viscera, the ligament,
the before time and never again.

An intake of breath, quick, like a gunshot.

Witness Anne Marie in her hospital gown
(Zippy to her friends), heart working overtime
to move the extra blood through her body.

Veins branching outward in the general direction
of "away." Never quite making it. There's no escaping

the circulatory system—it pulls the blood back in and cycles it.

Our love repeated, or else an elegant system.
Without it the lungs, the lungs are just hollowed-out
wing flesh feeding nothing and no child forming.

(Wings are everywhere in this story, if you're looking for them.)

But why wouldn't we
be looking for them here
in the canyon is not canyon, but sound?

.

ON THE DAY HE WAS BORN THE SKY LOOKED LIKE THIS:

Related because, according to us, "planet" is just another way of saying how things wander off but find their way again. Here, this concept of orbit is translated as "fate."

AS A COPPER MINE DREAMS OF SURFACING

Defining, yet underreported moments in the early years of Robert Craig Knievel, Jr.:

1954 (age sixteen)— Our hero takes his first job as a diamond drill operator with the Anaconda Mining Company. Decides the earth has nothing for him.

1957 (age nineteen)— Our hero joins the military track team, specializing in pole-vaulting. Breaks no records, breaks no bones. False starts.

THE DEATH OF ROBERT CRAIG KNIEVEL, JR.

A rebel   vectoring   a terrible   rocket   a trick   orbiting
center   leveling   rock   a broken   cover   convert
reborn   a blink   in orbit   or clever   king   a biker   like
a kite   or let to linger   brave   center   reeling   gentler

Reborn as Evel, we hear: veil, shovel, devil.

CAESAR'S PALACE, 1967

Trajectory /n/: from the Latin *traiectus*,
past participle of the verb *traicere*. "Thrown across, thrown over."

> On final approach the universe
> splits in two, branching Y-like,
> arms outstretched
> to accommodate each outcome.

Knievel clears the fountains but does not stick the landing; in the morning the papers will describe the fall as end over end.

> $t \to \infty$, see in the sign
> for infinity, two worlds
> so close they look like an embrace.

Later, when asked how it feels to be in a coma for more than a month: *How the fuck should I know? I was in a coma.*

OR ELSE PICTURE THE CURVE AT THE NAPE OF A NECK

Whether or not he is aware of it, Evel
Knievel has attained terminal velocity.

> An object dropped from a high place.
> Neglect air resistance.
> Its velocity (v) after (t) seconds is given
> v=-32t feet per second.

On the other hand, when Knievel falls,
arms and legs spread wide
(or else a parachute),
resistance has a significant effect on the velocity.

Eventually the Δ v is less and less and reaches a constant value.
When graphed it makes an arc:

PITY THE COMET ITS SLOW DESCENT

Or the fact that it only appears to be falling.

MERIDIAN IDAHO, 1968

Fear of falling now nothing more than phantom:
the same thirteen cars, the same Triumph Bonneville.

>   Meridian /n/:
>   A circle of constant
>   longitude passing though
>   a given place on the earth.
>
>   Or else, a set of pathways   along the body,
>   a moving point, adrift without anchor
>   (rephrase: Knievel is at his zenith).

Statistically speaking, he's likely to make it.

They didn't come to see him die, but
then again, they knew about Caesar's, knew about Scottsdale,

were they disappointed to see him stick the landing, then?
No more bones ground down to dust?

HOUSTON ASTRODOME, 1971

Ten thousand tickets, a record set.
Here is grit. Here is grift. Heroic bait
for reckless spectators:
                                  the last
                                  great gladiator.
Perfect if you like
your heroes with a shoulder cape
and a little bit of leather.

Here's nothing more than
kinetic consequence.
Dare him, dare him and he'll jump
the dome itself.

COW PALACE, 1972

Our hero: slick, quick witted:
I don't even dream much.
How 'bout he does it twice.
He's on a collision course.

```
        *           *
            *    *
                *
```

Seen from below the stars
& stripes are so
small—a slight abrasion
across his chest—

as he crashes into the concessions,
a constellation of one.

SKY CYCLE

He wants
    propulsion.

He wants
    to build it.

He wants
    to have it built.

He wants
    the tumble of bodies.

He wants
    muscle memory of first flight.

He wants
    to spit in the face of something.

He wants
    you to buy his new album because

He wants
    to build it.

He wants
    it shaped like a bottle of beer.

He wants
>   it to fly but—

He wants
>   two back-up systems.

He wants
>   red and blue, alternately.

He wants
>   what he wants.

He wants
>   to build it.

He wants
>   to stop wanting.

He wants
>   to split the difference between here and the heavens.

He wants
>   to don a white suit and wax parabolic.

He wants
>   to be exiting your line of sight over and over again.

He wants
        to build it.

He wants
        to land it.

"GOOD LUCK WITH YOUR UNDERTAKING"

was all the note from the government said.
Quoth Knievel: *Undertaking is a damn lousy choice of words.*

HE WAS EVER SOME SORT OF SCAFFOLDING ON THE SKY

Consider for a moment that the earth did not want Knievel.
    He was never really here.

> Think of it this way: the g-force
> acting on stationary object Evel Knievel (EK)
> is 1 g, a result of the Earth's surface bearing upwards
> equal and opposite to gravity (gn) 9.80665 meters per
>   second squared.

1 g pushing him away sans launch.

Who better, then, to hold the heavens up?

SNAKE RIVER CANYON, 1974

Of course the fall.

A pedal, hell-bent. Maybe two.
From the ground it looks like a man
from the sky—we could not say.

The motion of an object   thrown up against itself
                                              (rephrase: we didn't look away).

The last thing we saw
before the parachute:
a plume, puff of smoke up into dust.

Caught up by the wind
He drifted back to where he began.

Round as orbit, an eye socket,
a cavity, land.

WEMBLEY, 1975

If it had only been twelve busses
Knievel would have made it, but twelve

doesn't have the same ring.
Fractured pelvis, broken hand.

Another intake of breath
as the stretcher is dismissed.

I came in walking, I went out walking,
a series of tiny vaults they will not fault.

As a father teaches his infant son,
ambulation is a controlled fall.

Launch yourself off balance and pray
the parabola doesn't come up short.

Knievel taught little Bobby more
than how to walk—he gave him wings,

or rather, beat them out of him
with a cane hollowed out to hold Wild Turkey.

Now Bobby does the warm-up show,
his face a softer, more attractive version

of his father's. His skin is smooth and pink
as new scar tissue. He always lands his jumps.

KING'S ISLAND, 1975

I can't do that, our hero said
upon his arrival at the scene.

I can't do that, he said,
when they offered to shorten the jump.

Give him eleven skydivers
jumping from 13,500 feet
to spell out the initials E.K.

> their potential energy
> (mass x gravity x height)
> converted back to kinetic.

Give him Frank Gifford, frantic,
and a 52% market share.

Give him little Bobby, orbiting his dad
in a blue leisure suit.

Give him two more buses than Wembley
—and a jump he can't top.

Now give him the will to stop.

1977 SHARK JUMP

> Never mind that the man-eating killers
> advertised were a scant 13 lemon sharks
> flown in from Florida, limp and listless in their tank.

A 90-minute spot in prime time is
still a fair leap from headlining a tractor pull.

The sum of all forces acting on a body isn't lift, it's will.
How else to explain this propulsion in the face of anatomy,
this wingless flight?

> He has segment, has arrows (has a vertebrae
> of arrows), has forelimbs, has a critical component
> of the flight system, has an actual number and still no
> more than ornament.

If he cannot be a passerine, Knievel will be a shark.

> Never mind that the cameraman
> injured during the practice run wipe out
> was treated for minor injuries and released,
> he didn't "have an eye gouged out."

We were in on the con, we only came
to watch him pick our pockets.

WITH APOLOGIES TO SHELLY SALTMAN

The FBI file on Knievel has grown to 290 pages, a minority in reference to the time our hero broke both your arms with an aluminum baseball bat.

P.S.—He's only going to serve a six month sentence.

P.P.S.—While you'll win a $12.75 million judgement against him in civil court, he's going to declare bankruptcy and will never pay you a dime.

REMEMBERING ALWAYS THAT THE LAST TWO FRACTURES WERE OBTAINED ON THE GOLF COURSE AND IN THE BATH

skull	fractured
nose	
teeth	
jaw	
clavicles	left and right
sternum	
arms	left and right
upper back	twice
lower back	twice
pelvis	crushed
pelvis	fractured (three times)
right hip	ball and socket replaced
right knee	
right shin	
toes	
right femur	five times
wrists	left and right
all ribs	fractured at least once

CLUTCH

He will also be very missed by sidekick "Rocket," his pet Maltese

Here's when it's time to disengage:

the space leant him
is anxious to be space again.
He feels the old gone feeling—

beneath the tongue there is a quickening.

Here's what Knievel knows:
how to rewrite the landscape by virtue
of his absence from it

so all that can be seen is all that is missing.

But let's say his fists
were balled (not to strike, but grip)
in a last holding—

what did he grasp after?

thicket, no	ricochet, no
throttle, no	torque, no
rocket:	that's what.

A rocket is a vehicle/vessel

of change, of thrust. The loyalty
of most things is in their honesty
in departing. Like everything,

Rocket was dying from his first lick.

But Knievel signed up to love
a passing thing—frenetic spark
that warmed a lap while idling.

What became of Rocket, after?

~~~~~~~~*~~~~~~~~~~~*
~~~~~~~~~~~*~~~*
~~~~~~~~~~~~~*

A number of birds hatched together
who will disperse never think whether
it's better to leave the nest first or be left.

NOTES AND ACKNOWLEDGMENTS

Earlier versions of the following poems appeared in *DIAGRAM* Issue 10.1:

Of the Items Necessary:
On the Night He Was Born the Sky Looked Like This
As a Copper Mine Dreams of Surfacing
The Death of Robert Craig Knievel, Jr.
Caesar's Palace, 1967
Or Else Picture the Curve at the Nape of a Neck
Snake River Canyon, 1974
Remembering Always that the Last Two Fractures were
    Obtained on the Golf Course, and in the Bath

The title page image is a popular diagram of the distribution of impact locations on motorcycles and is commonly attributed to accident researcher Dr. Dietmar Otte.

With sincere gratitude to my family and the MFA faculty at George Mason University, who read early drafts of many of these poems.

EMILY VIGGIANO SALAND is a graduate of the MFA program at George Mason University. Her poetry has appeared in *DIAGRAM*, *Smartish Pace*, *The Cincinnati Review*, *Radar Poetry*, *The Seneca Review*, and elsewhere. She works at Marist College in Poughkeepsie, NY.

✣

COLOPHON

Text is set in a digital version of Jenson, designed by Robert Slimbach in 1996, and based on the work of punchcutter, printer, and publisher Nicolas Jenson. The titles here are in Futura.

❉

NEW MICHIGAN PRESS, based in Tucson, Arizona, prints poetry and prose chapbooks, especially work that transcends traditional genre. Together with DIAGRAM, NMP sponsors a yearly chapbook competition.

DIAGRAM, a journal of text, art, and schematic, is published bimonthly at THEDIAGRAM.COM. Periodic print anthologies are available from the New Michigan Press at NEWMICHIGANPRESS.COM.

www.ingramcontent.com/pod-product-compliance
Lightning Source LLC
Chambersburg PA
CBHW031508040426
42444CB00007B/1249